TANGIANNA SAINT ALEIS

Calm in Calamity

Tangianna Saint Aleis

ISBN (Print Edition): 978-1-09830-939-8

ISBN (eBook Edition): 978-1-09830-940-4

In loving Memory of my Grandma Aleis

December 17, 1936 to December 26, 2009

My grandmother screamed, "Dear God! Who did this to you?" I rushed from my bedroom to discover my older sister Kiki covered in blood, crying, shaking, and barefoot. A man that we've never seen before answered, "I got them off her." It was maybe five girls beating and robbing her. I couldn't find my words; they were suppressed by my tears. How did this beating lead to two mild mannered pre-teen sisters en route to the hospital? Multiple chipped teeth, busted lip, swollen jaw, throbbing rib cage and dizziness from being stomped in the head. Younger by two years, I was scared, sad, most of all angry. Livid because I wasn't there to protect my best friend. I was reared with a very large diverse middle-class family. My mother gave birth to my sister while she was in college. My grandparents took her in as their own. My mother saw that as a green light to continue the partying. She gave birth to me two years later.

She was working, studying, and partying full time. Urban legend says the lifestyle the expecting mother creates the child's characteristics. My mother is one of 10 children; our own little tribe that throws amazing parties and then praises the Lord.

Many grandchildren came after us but we are the OG's. That's right original grandchildren. My aunt Charlena taught me how to read at three years old. My first book was *The Children's Sunday School* book. My sister and I sang in the church choir. Rehearsal was hours upon hours every Saturday. We went to a big church with a well-known pastor. My grandmother was on several committees at church. I enjoyed church. At a very young age, I picked up on the politics of the church. My father was a very handsome man in med school. He bought lots of things for my sister and me. One day, my mom and dad had a huge fight and I never saw him again. I was 5 years old. Never really felt the bond with my father. My grandmother Aleis, a beautiful multiracial import from Arkansas, and my grandfather, a tall, thin, chiseled face man from Mississippi, had 10 children. One being my mother; the other nine was the village that helped rear my sister and me.

This dynamic made us socially mature. We were always encouraged to be ourselves and not to follow others. I expressed myself through what I wore: my hair styles, art, and dance. I never set out to set trends. When the kids began to wear what I wore, I was over it. I would genuinely get bored. Eccentricities brings on teasing and bullying. Deep down inside, our critics are also fans.

Legends can't be recreated; only imitated and once that's realized, they're hated. My grandmother Aleis exuded glamour. Her skin naturally glowed. Her walk commanded attention. Her kindness, humor, amazing singing voice, and gift for writing garnered her a lot of admirers. She also gained quite a few foes. Her fashion sense threw them over the edge. If you got it, flaunt it. If they hate you for it, they want it. On my first day of school for kindergarten, she dressed me in a pink dress, white tights, white silk socks with pearls around the ankle, pink patent shoes, and a fur jacket. The kids would fight to sit next to me at lunch and play with me at recess. The little girls began to wear everything I wore. School work was easy to me, almost too easy to the point of boredom. Every year, we'd take comprehension and math state exams and I was always several grades ahead. I finally took an IQ test and scored well. I garnered a love of arts and technology from my Aunt Bobbie and Uncle Terry: visiting museums as well as creating and enjoying music. One of my earliest memories is break dancing at a party. A full-on circle of people around me, I embark on my helicopter move. Suddenly, I wake up drenched in water. I passed out. First time partying too hard and I was only six! My eldest Uncle Eddie knew everyone at the nightclubs, lounges, arcades, and everywhere cool. His son was 11 months younger than me. We would all hang out. Not how most kids are raised. My cousin, sister, and I would play video games and race go karts during the day. At night, my uncle would take us to listen to house music at clubs, jazz lounges, and cool neon arcades, It was awesome!! I also spent a lot of time with my Uncle Derrick, who was a bit quieter and more into games and books that were intellectually stimulating. We would spend hours reading about the *Myng Dynasty*, *The Art of War*, and Machiavelli. We would spend a whole day playing Monopoly.

My sister and I went to school to learn. We didn't feel the need to fit in. The "cool kids" were not cool to us. Bullying ensues when people who feel like you're rejecting them admire you. We simply had a strict upbringing that didn't allow time for socializing. Kids took it personal and it got pretty bad so bad that my aunt Mona would have to pick us up in her car 1 block away. It didn't help that it was the Night Rider car. No, really she had a vehicle duplicated from the tv show. My classmates would surround it and try to make it talk. My later years in junior high, I was kicking asses and taking names. I knew I was smarter and better than that. I joined basketball, floor hockey, and cheer-leading. I exercised my comedic muscle to put my peers at ease around me. As a preteen, I read the Bible a lot and didn't hide that. Being labeled the "holy roller"was fine with me. People started to leave the holy roller alone. Something about spirituality creeps most kids out. I was naturally evolving into a stronger person that looked toward my spirituality for answers. The summer I was entering junior high, my whole family was over to the house eating and having a great time. My mom bought my Uncle Eddie some cool shoes and he loved them. We laughed all night. Eddie got up Friday morning for work. Saturday and Sunday came and went with no sign of Eddie. Monday passed and he didn't show up for work. Wednesday afternoon, the phone rang. The coroner called for the family to come in and identify the body. He died of a cocaine overdose. The entire family was devastated.

My sister was enrolled in high school and I was wrapping up junior high as we rode to the hospital with my grandmother. She vowed to move us out of the inner city and into the suburbs. Two hours and a couple hundred miles away, our family mapped out a plan that would optimize our potential and diversify our surroundings, most importantly keeping us out of harm's way. First day of school, my 35-year-old Uncle Terry took my sister and me to school. He looked extremely young for his age and very muscular due to his workout routine. My mom bought me my first Chanel bag and new clothes to start high school.

My mom has a very kind heart and never had a problem getting on her feet; she just never ran to her kids. As I stumbled to my locker with what seemed like 20 books, a backpack of supplies, my business skirt, button down blouse, model older sister, and rippled muscled Uncle Terry, we made quite the entrance.

In homeroom, a girl that resembled me sat next to me and introduced herself as Daisy. I became aware of Daisy's popularity very quickly. I received the complete rundown of the different cliques, best lunch hours, parties and events to attend and not to attend. She was one grade older than me: stood about 5'5", biracial (black mother and white father), wild curly hair, and glasses. Daisy's older sister Donna was in the same grade as my sister. Their older cousin Doug was 6'5", an all-state wrestler and football star destined for success and gorgeous. Daisy's family history lesson came to an end as the homeroom bell rang. This guy approached us; she introduced me to Doug, her cousin. I get to lunch and nervously scan my surroundings. Then I hear, "Let me introduce you to my cousin." The table full of teenagers who looked like mini adults. Her boyfriend Mike, an honors student and aspiring singer, softly introduced himself. His best friend was in a hip-hop group and they all traveled in unison. Word quickly spread about a party Friday night at Doug's house. Daisy turned to me as I was leaving lunch and asked "You're coming, right"? "Yeah, for sure. Can my sister come too?" I asked, of course she replied.

My sister and I were dropped off at this beautiful home on Friday night with endless Benzes and beamers in the driveway leading down to the street. The party was packed and loud. I introduced my sister to my new friends. I also quickly locked eyes with two puppy dog eyes, chiseled face smooth caramel-skin boys with teeth whiter and straighter than Chiclets. I kept telling myself "Smile and look away. Smile and look away." I was staring at him unintentionally. Who is he? What school does he attend? How old is he? I needed answers!

Mike's hip hop friends were attracted to my sister like bees to honey. My older sister did some modeling. She's tall, thin, naturally busty, and beautiful and yet quiet and shy. She often got mistaken for being stuck up. The night was winding down. Daisy, Mike, and an unidentified young man were in the kitchen. Daisy excitedly waved me over. "I want you to meet Bill, Mike's younger brother. He's a freshman like you." Bill was soft spoken and adorable, extremely well-mannered and intelligent. I told him a bit about my background and my thoughts on my new environment. Bill mentioned some places and things to check out: the downtown riverwalk and the beautiful cathedrals a few towns over. We exchanged phone numbers. I wanted to thank Doug for having my sister and me over. However, I didn't see him the entire night. We made our exit and called it a night. Daisy yelled, "See you guys next week! Same time! Same place!"

I couldn't wait to tell my grandmother all about my happenings. I was so excited like my sister and I finally felt we found our squad. My grandmother was happy yet cautious. She advised me to focus on my studies, find a Christian church nearby, and hold tight to our values. Work hard in youth so you can bear the fruit in adulthood. A slightly more intense conversation than expected. This reminded me of the time I was in first grade and getting in line after recess. Sheldon, the cutest boy in class, was the only kid I've ever seen with smoldering blue and yellow eyes, not hazel yellow. His older brother came over and shouted, "Who is Tangianna?" I said me. He smirked and gave me a big bag of assorted candies and snacks and said this is from my brother Sheldon. I was so happy. I told my grandmother Aleis and she quickly replied to go do your homework. "I'm not going to allow you to be young and pregnant like your mother." I was seven years old. Oddly enough, Sheldon became a father at 15 years old.

I arrived at school scared and motivated an hour early on Monday to study. As I was walking to my locker, I couldn't believe my eyes. Mr. Chiclet aka the hot guy who I locked eyes with at the party. His locker was right across from mine. I was at my locker.

He starts moving in my direction. His 6'1" frame was gliding towards me. I played it cool adjusting some books. I looked back up and he glided right past me to my locker neighbor Robert. This carried on for 2 months. Robert and I became friendly exchanging little jokes. One day, I had several items spread in front of his locker. They both came over laughing. Robert stated he was going to have to charge me rent for occupying so much space. "How much is rent?" "You must give Adam your phone number. He has a name and it's Adam!" I ripped off a piece of notebook paper and gave him my name and number and prayed for the best. LOL

I went through the rest of my day wondering when or if he was going to call. After school, I began to drown my anxieties in a strawberry smoothie. My phone rang. A deep voice replies to my hello in a deep hi. "This is Adam. How are you?" We talked. Turns out he was an older man, a senior that recently broke up with his college freshman girlfriend. That's like a high school scandal. We talked for hours and had so many things in common. We decided to grab something to eat that Friday evening.

We went to a cute restaurant not too far from school. We also went to the school football game and watched the second half. We were winning. Doug was on fire; no one was getting past him. We won. We partied again at Doug's beautiful estate. Adam didn't seem to want to go, which I found odd because that's where I first laid eyes on him. I asked about the sudden mood change. He told me he didn't want me to attend this party or any future parties here. "Why?" "I'll show you." We entered through a different door at Doug's to a small house attached to the bigger one. The door opened to music playing loudly, kids partying in a more nestled setting. The kitchen had liquor and every counter was covered in narcotics. There were cake dishes of cocaine, industrial size jars of marijuana. Pills, pills, and more pills. I just wanted to run out of there. I knew my sister and I did not move to Middle of Babylon, IL to engage in activities such as these. I just buried my beloved Uncle Eddie to drug abuse. I know how badly this could go and wanted no part of it. We left bullets and bullies to deal with kids addicted to blow and Benzes. There are obstacle courses everywhere. You can't run; you can only deal with it head on.

I just say no, enjoy the music, and make my exit to never return. Remain friendly in passing. Adam dropped me off at home and we continued to date. He was close to his parents. I began to go to church with him and his mother. He finally asked me to his prom. There was one big problem! I wasn't allowed to have a boyfriend until I was 16 years old. Going to prom at 14 with a 17 year old was a big NO. I had to watch the boy I adored go to prom with another girl.

My sister and I went to New York and Canada for most of the summer. Adam and I saw each other when I was home for summer for two weeks and went our separate ways. He went off to college. My sister was starting her senior year; I just wanted to get it all over with. Doug and my sister had two classes together. He would invite her to his house for his infamous shindigs. She obliged religiously. He wasn't used to hearing no. Mr. All-State, Mr. Popular.

Doug didn't show up for class one Monday. The whispers quickly travelled through the hall that Doug got arrested for murder. This kid had everything: A beautiful family, well-to-do parents, a promising collegiate career in his future with a guaranteed full ride scholarship from wrestling and football. Doug had a volatile temper that matched his ego with a hard-core substance abuse habit. That was a recipe for a life sentence for murdering someone over a verbal disagreement.

My high school was huge and beautiful. It was mostly glass like 60 percent of the architectural structure, so it was always bright and sunny. The vitamin D was amazing for the students and staff. I met great friends from all around the world. We got a lot of imports because our town was ranked top 10 in the country to live and raise a family, number 1 in Illinois.

The girl who played forward on her junior high hockey team and point guard was no more. I tucked away my collectors cards. I still had the love of sports but now as a spectator. With a nurse note in tow and sitting in the bleachers in gym class, I felt a tap on my shoulder and an upbeat voice asked loudly "Who cuts your hair?" I turned around and replied, "Nadine. She's a two-hour drive away from me." "You drive two hours to get your hair styled?" "Well did you not just take notice and inquire about it?" I replied with a giggle. "Touché." She replied."My hairstylist is not too far from my old neighborhood. I'm new to the school." "Me too! I live three minutes away, but my younger sister and I just transferred here this year." "Really? From where?" "A boarding school in England." I wanted to ask why so but didn't want to intrude. "What period is your lunch?" "After PE." "Mine too." "I'll come with you. Ok, cool." "Why haven't I ever seen you in PE or my lunch before?" "I'm around," she answered vaguely. I knew my spidey sense would get to the bottom of it. The parallel in our life was so uncanny. I could tell she needed a friend. She told me all about her native country India and the origin of her name Isa. Isa was a first-generation immigrant whose parents were super successful entrepreneurs. We were both upbeat and excited for each other to meet each other's sister. Isa and I declared to participate in gym and eat healthier. I created the workout slogan "Grow gold not old!" We developed a bond over the fear of getting chubby. I soon found out she was diabetic, which really shocked me due to my ignorance of the disease. Our health lifestyle change was fun yet essential. "Hey, my older sister's friend is having a concert this weekend. You and your sister should come."

We meet up with Isa's sister. I immediately noticed they were night and day. Total opposites. Isa was outgoing and transparent while Juliann was meek not weak, a silent riot type. She found comfort with my sister and I due to the bond we formed with her sister. However, outside of that she judged everyone and everything harshly and voice her disdain rapidly and frequently. This was not how she presented herself to the world. They were both pretty, Juliann came across kind and shy and began to build a deeper rapport with my sister. We became a sibling gang: we did everything together and hung out at each other's homes constantly. Her parents took us around everywhere until we learned how to drive. Their father was tough as nails. He scolded us one time for going to a haunted house on Halloween that he deemed demonic and didn't want us to burn in Hell. Isa and I joined an organization at the neighborhood church that funded and created orphanages in third world countries. We finessed them to focus on the Middle East and began to do the leg work. It felt amazing working to help others.

Juliann was waiting for a ride home one evening. She decided to catch a ride with a few of the guys from the hip hop group. She says they sexually assaulted her. She returned home, showered, and told her mother who called authorities. This all happened so fast that my sister fed me the news from a source other than Isa and Juliann. This was so bizarre as they were just over to our house a few days ago. I called to make sure every-thing was fine and praying to God this was all a rumor. Their father answered the phone and angrily said they couldn't come to the phone and hung up. A few days later, Isa called and asked us to come over. She didn't say much over the phone and said she didn't want to cause she couldn't. We went over there and right away noticed a change in the parents' behavior towards us. Isa confirmed what everyone was saying was true. Kiki was so shocked: these guys were her friends and Juliann was her friend. This seemed so out of character for these guys. They were always so pleasant and respectful. You must side with the victim until given a reason not to do so. Remember my spidey senses? I finally asked Isa why they left their school in England? After a sign that blew my hair back, Isa divulged that Julianna began dating a guy from a neighboring school. She fell in love and got pregnant. "My father made us return home and the baby was terminated." "Why are the accused free with no charges?"

Juliann's rape kit came back inconclusive. Isa said we're moving to New York. Our family has offices there and my dad is disgusted with this area now. The guys were never prosecuted or even charged. They denied all claims. We never saw Isa and Juliann again. My sister later told me Juliann said her true love was waiting for her in New York.

I wondered "Where did they end up? Are they still running? Will the truth ever set Juliann free?" Or, is she still charging a fee for every good deed and finessing her way onto everyone of her family member's life insurance policy? My older sister and I received shortened schedules from school and would spend our free time at Oakbrook Center. This place would take all our allowance and force me to get a part-time job. Kiki's senior year was closing, and I got transferred to honors English and was reunited with a familiar face, Bill!

Bill was an old soul. " A sommelier in the making" we would joke. He knew about different fine wines and loved architecture. His father was an engineer and his uncle was an architect. We became study partners and reader beaters that critiqued each other's paper's we essentially became inseparable friends. His older brother graduated the same year as Kiki. We all celebrated. This was a fun, emotional time, given everything Kiki had overcome we were all proud to see her graduate and go off to college.

Bill and I wanted in on the fun, so I took my Uncle Terry's car to Six Flags along with Bill. We hung out with friends until the closing parade. We got to the car and it wouldn't start. We tried everything as the parking lot cleared out so did the air in the front right tire…. The tow truck took hours to come. As we waited, our friendship deepened just by how nurturing and caring he was towards me yet still very calm and humorous. We remained friends throughout school and acquaintances in young adult life when he was going through internships at architect firms. He invited me to an architectural tour that really change my life and gave me a great appreciation for architectural design. I became obsessed with the history and different styles and techniques. I asked Bill about his current compensation. Bill told me the job was not paying, but a great experience. People who knew me would say I am an extrovert. I am a human conundrum because I don't say maybe 70% of the things I'm thinking unless asked. Not sure if that is healthy. That I do this. I seem to hurt people's feelings very easily without intent. I blame this on my Aquarius sun, Libra moon, and Venus in Capricorn. Example: my Venus in Capricorn wants to tell Bill "if it doesn't make dollars, it doesn't make sense!" My Aquarius sun wants to help others any way I can, including financially. My Libra moon says don't say anything since that may hurt his feelings or make things tense. Sometimes my sun wins, sometimes my moon, and other times my Venus.

I reached out to several architect firms in Chicago the summer after my senior year. I tailored my resume to the design industry. I got a call within a week for a studio director position at a major firm in downtown Chicago. The initial phone call was so brief. They said we're conducting interviews Thursday and Friday for our second round of interviews. However, we can see you Wednesday, tomorrow. "Shut the front door and open the back one." I had 11 hours to research and prepare. I studied the company background and design portfolio. I rehearsed answers to common interview questions. I put together the perfect power ensemble and got a good night's rest. A nice big cup of ginger tea with honey and my nightly prayers had me sleep like a pacified baby.

Awaken by the morning sun and the sound of snow dropping on my window, I got dressed in a gray skirt suit with a white shirt crispier than a knife. I drove into Chicago through a snowstorm. Shivering, I took the elevator up to the swanky office. I approached the peppy brunette receptionist and asked for Ramona. Ramona came out from behind a huge wall that slid open to reveal a huge studio filled with offices. She stood about 6 feet tall, thin, blonde with small features. She reached out to shake my hand. I shook it and she jumped back because my hands were so cold. We went back to her office and went right into her questions. "So, tell me about yourself." The first thing that came to my mind: "I can eat my body weight in shrimp, I love night strolls on the beach, and men in three-piece suits." Her serious demeanor quickly cracked, and she laughed out loud. After she gained her composure, she looked at me and said no. Seriously it was that easy. She said tell me about yourself. I blurted out "I'm motivated and inspired by design and look-ing for a company to grow together with from the ground up." Ramona said she was a former model who also tried her hand in acting and ended up in human resources. She wanted to suc-ceed in entertainment but that didn't pan out. Plan C, D or E not sure where she was in the alphabet. "Why do you want to work here?" "I'm going to be frank with you. No, I will be Francine." Ramona laughed out loud again. "Architectural interior design has piqued my interest in a major way and knowing that there is a window of opportunity at Bonjour Architecture. I want to create and make it my home. I am such a design enthusiast that I specifically told the employment agency that sent me here that

I was solely interested in the design field. And the best way to know 100% if this is indeed my career heart calling is to get in the actual atmosphere." She nodded in agreement and quickly shot at me. "Tell me about your weaknesses?" "Strawberry ice cream, guys with six packs who love their mothers, white fluffy puppies." She stopped me during her laughter and in what was a laugh scream and said professional weakness. "I make my work my passion and I get tunnel vision and other parts of my life suffer. This is my passion and I am willing to start from the ground up and work my way up brick by brick."

I got the job. This job is extreme to do. I seek and schedule accredited lunch and learns, keep track and manage the firm's AIA credits, petty cash, and things of that nature. They had a stunning office on Michigan Avenue right between Louis Vuitton and the Chanel Boutiques. Floor to ceiling windows, open modern space with futuristic metal and Parisian accents. The sun beamed through its magnificent sculpture. My area was in between the interior of the company, overseen and owned by my boss's wife Janice. She had a team of five and they were fabulous and very nice.

The architects had a more understated fashion sense. What they lacked in garb they made up for it in gab. They also have the most creative minds.

My sister was studying child psychology at a private university in the city. Her books became my bedtime reads. As much as I love design, the mechanical makeup of the mind is my biggest wonder. My IQ has been recorded above average several times and no curriculum was able to hold my attention for an extended amount of time. The parallels between physics and spirituality intrigued me. Its strong nature supported my faith and beliefs in higher unknown to some but recognized by many including myself as God. The law of attraction quantifies hope, prayer and faith. One has their desire; they present it to their God, and they proceed to work on the manifestation. The hospitality of the universe strongly depends on the action we put into motion. Manifestation is into action. Prayer without work is just a wish. True believing may cause some bleeding. No, some forces can't be seen. The wind pushes us and yet is naked to sight questions of the lord never took residence in my mind whenever conversations on spirituality with intellects and self-proclaim genius. Theory proven by other humans is always helpful; that in half has always amazed me how some are massively highbrow but lack the confidence to make the executive decision over their own thoughts. I can be charitable in Chanel, blast Tupac followed by Tony Bennett, and tightrope between school of life or curriculums that could not hold my attention.

I was sitting between an architectural rock and in the interior of a hard place. One spring a year and a half after I started at Bonjour, I was sent to Merchandise Mart, a large beautiful trade mall formally owned by the Kennedys, with Jax the only male interior designer in the studio. We've already exchanged pleasantries and looked forward to getting out of the office. Silks and leather were our buffet items that would later be selected and upholstered after learning its origin and treatment. One brand solely makes leather and furs from animals that died of natural causes. Silk lace imported from Italy made by a mother and daughter duo.

Jax was tall with a slender blond bob haircut. An Indiana import, he shared over lunch details of his childhood as a gay boy in rural Midwest America. Lunch and learns soon became a weekly routine. This dynamic continued for about a year. At this point, I began taking interior design courses. Jax was stoked about his newly installed bar and booth and insisted that I come over to toast our newness. I soon discovered his house was more fabulous than I anticipated. Beautiful circular driveway with a fountain as the centerpiece. The foyer was breathtaking skylight aluminous. Décor inspired by old Hollywood. This place was just shy of a pair of shoulder pads of being called Joan Crawford. It was gorgeous and glamorous. Compliments and cheers were exchanged, conversations turned to our love lives. I divulged about the current guy I've been dating on/off for 3 years. Jax said "We got nothing but time and wine to kill." He's tall, handsome, ranked in the top 10 college baseball players. He is humble yet not mentally stimulating. He can feel me moving on because that's when he reaches out when I meet a new guy. His game was on ESPN last week and I heard a girl cheering him on "Great job babe and woot baby." Jax jokingly mocked me and told me run don't walk away from this guy.

All the men my age seemed to be game players. "We must find you another or has he already found you? What about Mr. Nichols? The old man that owns the engineering firm. Yes, he always asks about you and not in a professional manner." "What? Expound?" "When you're not around I hear him asking Ramona or Frances where are you?" "Tell her I said 'Hi.'" "Well, I clean my ears with Q-tips. I don't date them. I am happy and in love with a 'Q-tip' and as soon as gay marriage is legalized, we will marry!" "Details, Jax!" "He's the owner of a championship sports team and he's not in the closet or out. He is good to me and I know he loves me. His position's profession is hyper masculine." "Does it bother you to live a secret?" "I live a private life. I choose whom I share my personal life with. I see where this world is headed. Oversharing and not enough caring." It was getting late and I had to bid Jax a farewell and get home to my courses well into the night.

When my phone buzzed to awaken me, it was Carlos inviting me to Miami where he played baseball. I accepted but desperately needed a change with this situation or a completely new relationship. Whatever I was feeling, I knew this wasn't it, so I prayed to God to fix it in the best way possible. I landed in Miami and Miami was Miami. Hot, sexy, sweaty and shallow. We had drinks, danced, and went for a long walk on the beach. I told him we cannot be intimate until we are committed. He promised our relationship would change for the better once he got drafted. We took our shoes off and walked into the ocean, stared intensely at each other, and kissed. I woke up in his arms that morning. He tells me we are going on a friend's boat. Well, just great I didn't bring the proper shoes. I went to the store to buy flats and left him behind. When I arrived at the store by foot, I realized my wallet was not in my handbag. I u-turned and beelined back to the room and guess who is not there. I searched and searched to no recovery. I called him to no avail. I called the front desk and housekeeping. I was so hurt and angry. I immediately phoned my older sister and erupted. A walk was needed to clear my head and lower my blood pressure. I was mad at myself a lot of signs were pointing to clown town with this guy and I don't partake in circuses. I made up my mind not to call the cops. Have my

passport overnighted to me and never talk to this guy again. I sat in the sun and a sense of peace entered me and I looked up to the sky and thought "It's Handled." Wasn't the ending I anticipated but it was no coming back from that. Door closed; door bolted. Not until these sheets has anyone besides three people heard this story. My sister, Jax and we'll get to the third person in just a second.

Back home, Jax invited me to a game and after party. I accepted and desperately needed to have a good time. We got a table next to some players and their companions. After awhile, a young lady with blonde hair, olive skin, and a heavy Spanish accent approached our table and said "Who are you all? Everyone seems to know you and you're the best dressed in the club." We introduced ourselves and she introduced herself. She was the fiancée of one of the players and that my friends are the understatement of the century. We joined her eclectic table of friends and partied into the wee hours of the night. It wasn't long before

I ran into that same fiancée while out Christmas shopping. We spoke briefly and once again she complimented my style and asked for my input on her scarf and handbag combination. I instructed her to select warm Hermes bags and highlight them with bright Hermes scarfs. She loved it! And bought them all. I was on lunch and had to bid a farewell and hightail back to work. Before I could sit down, François called me into his office, sat me into his office, sat me down and closed the door. At this point I'm freaking out on the inside backtracking thinking "what did I F up"? "How do you like it here," he said in his heavy accent? "Very much." "How is your coursework coming along?" "Slow and steady." "Well, a lot of my clients speak very highly of you and their interactions with you. My wife and I like that in you and would like for to sit in all interior focused lunch and learn sessions." Oh my God! "Of course, I would love that! Thank you so much." I get to my desk. There is a business card under my key-board. Nichols Engineer and Construction! "Call me" handwritten in Sharpie. I put the card in my handbag. I needed a moment to gather myself from the eventful afternoon. I had to share all this with the coolest person on the planet: my grandmother Aleis. She gave me the latest family news, her lunch menu, church updates, and age life wisdom. A little time had passed, and Mr. Nichols comes into the office. He was a very well-dressed man, stood about 5'8" with salt and pepper hair and a very jolly disposition. He walked over to me after his meeting and jokingly said he was angry with me for not calling him. I apologized and finally accepted to go out that following Friday. On Friday, he picked me up and we went to a swanky Japanese restaurant where I learned about his Greek background and childhood in Boston. His birthday was the day after my mother's and my birthday was the day before his mother's! Our sense of humors and values were very similar. Something was happening. At the end of the date, he leaned in for a kiss and it was electric. He described it as an electric cord between us. We ended the night on that high note. I kept the two promises made to grandma: don't take the old man dancing and never tell your colleagues you're dating. He called and we had a lunch date at a steak house about a 20-minute drive away. Whenever I didn't have a lunch and learn and his schedule permitted, we were together. He was previously married but had been divorced for 10 years.

My phone rings; a young lady asks to speak with me. "Speaking." She stated that she got my contact information from Jocelyn {an acquaintance we mutually knew}, the fiancée earlier mentioned. She introduced herself as Susan, the wife of a newly traded player. She was looking for an interior designer and heard wonderful things about my style. I was obviously flattered.

About 3 weeks later, I begin my monthly payable and receivable account report. I noticed a new job with a lot of high expenses -- all projects were named by address. I could play Inspector Gadget or simply dial the phone number. I did the latter. Phone rings and rings and rings. A guy picks up the phone. I introduced myself and where I'm calling from and he cuts me off. "Please call Susan on her cell phone!" I get her mobile number from him even though I already had it. I called Susan and she answered right away. "Hi, it's Tangianna, how are you?" "I'm great!" "I really appreciate your hard work and the beautiful selections you sent me. "I sent you?" I asked. My mind went blank for 0.5 seconds. "Who have you had your face to face consultations with?" "Jax. He's been great with getting over your input." She replied. "You're so welcome, Susan. My apologies. Let me call you right back." I called Susan back to set up her next "go see" and confirmed the day, time, and me being present with Jax and my boss. Susan and I set the appointment for Thursday at 2pm. I literally skip to her office and knock on her door as she takes the call. She's smiling and talking. Hangs up the phone, looks at me, and asks me "How can she help me? Were you aware that Susan was under the impression I am involved in her project? Are you aware that Susan is a client here because of me?" "Yes and Yes." "Why am I just finding out and in this manner of 'detective work'?" Her face went pale and she danced on the letter S. It sounded like she was singing. Nothing she said made sense. I got up and went across the hall to Francois office and put in my 2 weeks notice. Time is the most valuable thing I can give love and honesty right on the heels. My time here was done. Bon voyage. I had to tell Susan the truth and grow from this betrayal. This was all fun and games until Jax felt threatened. Such a huge crack in his armor, insecurity amplified. A contact curator emerged from that young age. I obtained the contact phone number, personal and business, e-mail, social media, blood sample, and zodiac sign. I phoned Susan and told her everything. I offered to do her project for less money, or she could continue with Bonjour. To my surprise, she said, "Let's Go!" "Okay, great!" "I'll look at the space next week!" Mr. Nichols aka Nick was proud of me and appalled at the people that were still his clients.

Nick and I were eating quietly when he reached in his pocket and put a key on the table. He looked me in the eye and asked me to move in with him. We both wanted to go in a stable direction, but I wasn't expecting this so soon. I followed my heart and said yes! He had multiple homes. Settling into downtown seemed natural, a central location for both of us. I befriended Susan and completed some of the interior design and all of the decorating. I started making so many contacts from people wanting me to do interior design to simply style and give them fashion advice. Sometimes I didn't know how to charge someone for telling the round toe shoes and knee length skirts make them look chubby.

I've been working since I was 14 years old. At my young age, I realized I am the optimistic realist. I say my entire mindset had to be retrained to be more business savvy. Business boot-camp became my way of life. Everything from reading *The Art of War*, *48 Laws of Power*, watching *The Godfather*, *Citizen Kane* and shadowing Nick to meetings. I started brainstorming on how I could overcome what I needed the most work on negotiating the wheels in my head started turning and I compiled a list of activities and put myself in real life situations that called for me to negotiate.

Whether it was for yoga swag with my membership or 20% off at Neiman Marcups, oops, I mean Marcus. Haggling for free yoga mats got old quickly. We celebrated a friend's final days in the States before relocating back to Beirut. Ishmael was the man of the hour. There were about 15 of us, mostly family and close friends, starting off with drinks and dinner. Ishmael and I met in high school. He has olive skin, thinly built with almond shape chestnut and blue eyes. His wife was picked out for him at 21. He told his family he wasn't ready to settle down but they limited their financial support to the barest of necessities. He became a self-made millionaire through trading and investing at the age of 26. He stepped out on faith and made the decision to be a self-made Mack that doesn't plan on settling down until he is 60 years old (his words not mine). After dinner, we went dancing into the wee hours of the night. By this time, there were over 70 people. We didn't want the party to end. I invited some of the crew to my place. I lived right by the disco. Ishmael compliments the carbon fiber and leather walls in the front vanity bathroom and told me it reminded him of his Bugatti that he sold to a dealership the previous week. He had an ideal amount and contacted several luxury dealerships countrywide. One dealership came extremely close and became the owner of his Bugatti. What I found interesting was the negotiating process and financial spread. Wholesale value versus retail value. Ishmael told me the amount he sold his car and to what dealership. I watched this car appear online for sale and within weeks it was offline. I called that dealership to purchase the car and was informed it was sold. I asked the final selling price and he told me it sold for the asking price minus the shipping cost to the paying customer. It was an $80,000 markup! I found the negotiating outlet/practice I was looking for in luxury automotive industry.

In between my designing/styling orders and lifestyle blog I just started, I began to research the different luxury brands and the groups they were affiliated with and their history origin. I narrowed it down to three brands and proceeded with my research. First stop: Craigslist job listing. I typed in my first-choice brand. Like magic, the first post read "downtown luxury dealership seeking detail-oriented person with finance background. Apply within." I read this about 2 p.m.;I was dressed for a new position by 4 p.m. I claimed it mentally and presented myself as such. I wasn't cocky. Cockiness is a low vibration or confidence. We must always operate on a high vibration. I know confidence gets taxing especially with residuals from our past. I wore a black Armani pants suit, white crisp blouse, professional yet sexy, high heel pumps, and a gray fur coat casually tossed on my shoulders. (All furs worn by me died of natural causes.) I enter the establishment. Sales associates immediately greet me, asking if I need assistance. I decline and proceed to the older lady sitting at a huge glass circular reception area. I ask to speak with the general manager and owner son Tony Jr. She hands me paperwork to complete. I wait for about 15 minutes and he shows up with coffee in his hand, four finger grip, you know (pinky extended, standing over 6 feet tall, sturdy build, and very well dressed). We exchange pleasantries and step into a side office to conduct the interview. He looked over my resume for 5 minutes and asked me why I should hire you for my finance department? "I'm a hard worker. I live 10 minutes away and I'm detail oriented." We got up and he said "I'll be right back. I want you to meet someone." I sit in this office for what feels like an eternity as everyone who walks by peeks through the 360-degree, glass office, like standing in a fishbowl. I meet Jim, the finance director. Jim was a savvy firecracker who explained to me what would be needed from me and what the position truly entailed. It's like I had to get Tony Jr. approval first, the decision maker. I knew that right away. He was jovial yet alpha. I enjoyed our meeting. We talked about our travels and had similar senses of humor. When I was there about 2 1/2 hours, Nick called me asking where I was. The interview wrapped up and we bid each other farewells. I got to the door and turned my key at home when my Blackberry rang. A male voice asked "Are you a hard worker?" He repeated himself and I replied "Yes, I am!!" "Its's Tony Jr. and you're hired!" Nick met me at the door and he had no idea where I had been. I indulged Nick at first. He seemed indifferent. I explained the bigger picture of a great learning experience and excellent addition to my styling/designing and my blog.

My schedule started off like a country club: 1 p.m. to 7 p.m. Stage one was to shadow Jim from 10 a.m.- 5 p.m. to clean up his deals and make sure I pitch applicable maintenance and warranty coverage when Jim was not around. I got paid base and percentage of product. My new learning experience started Monday morning. He greeted me, got us coffee, took off his tailor-made Italian suit jacket, pulled me up a chair right next to him and said, "We got all night to work!" The first client flew in from Texas to purchase a Rolls Royce. He was a heavier man with a deep southern accent. Jim pulled some small talk out of him. They found common ground in fishing. Jim reiterated the value of his newly purchased vehicle and proceeded to tell him what he didn't need in vehicle insurance and cosmetic protection but insisted that it would be a financial lost not to purchase a gap warranty. Truth be told the only warranty you can put on a half a million dollar car is gap insurance. The customer took Jim's advice and hopped on a plane and had his car shipped to him. A father and son deal came in. Jim loaded the deal into the computer; within 10 minutes, they were purchasing a convertible BMW. for a 17-year-old kid. Jim made sure to mention his own teenage son and daughter. Jim told the duo about their extracurricular activities, their cars and all the vehicle insurance and cosmetic work they constantly need. If he had to pay out of pocket every single time, he'd be in the poor house. They bought everything he offered. This went on all day. I thought to myself, "how am I going to improve my negotiating skills?" He doesn't negotiate. He doesn't have to negotiate. The next morning, I get to the dealership around 10 a.m. to prepare and send the deals to the bank and back office. Jim is already there packaging the deals. He hands me a stack of little white slips with the deal name and a bonus amount. He paid me a percentage of every deal he did and that continued my duration working with him. I was getting my salary, commission, and Jim's bonuses. Down the road, I found out that just doesn't happen. Jim and I began to form a friendship; we'd laugh and joke all day. He would give me heads up and inside scoop on dealership politics. All the sales associates were friendly. Jim had a finance partner who essentially had the same responsibilities. I sat with him once and gave him pointers on how to be more personable and engaging. His name was Tom, a heavy-set guy about 6'2". He processed about 35% of the deals while Jim processed the rest. Tom was recently divorced with a teenage daughter and recently re-entered the online dating scene. My shadowing time was spent giving dating and photo angle advice. His voice was monotone, and he spent significantly more time with clients. What Tom lacked in vernacular and charm, he made up for it in patience and persistence. Tom closed almost every single deal that came across his desk. Jim and Tom processed over 300 vehicles per month. Training lasted a week.

I quickly began selling warranties ala carte and making sure all deals were funded in a timely manner.

I began to meet people from all nationalities, professions, personalities, and tax brackets. After a year, my boyfriend Nick, some friends and myself took a 2-week holiday to Cabo San Lucas, Mexico.

It was great fun, we ATVed through the mountains during the day and partied all night. On the way back home, I revealed to Nick that my period was late, which I found perplexing because I was on birth control pills. I was scared for several reasons. I wasn't ready to be a mother. No one in my family besides my sister and cousin have ever met Nick. He was old enough to be my father and in some parts of the world grandfather. Tanned and toned back from vacation, I got back to business and it didn't feel like work. We would all meet in Jim's office for laughs and lodging during downtime. Prior to starting my workday, I had an OBGYN appointment. I wasn't pregnant. My birth control pills were compromising my hormones. The doctor/gynecologist said I should switch brands right away.

That same week at the office, Jim tells me I will get more client time in the evenings on the day he leaves early. I was stoked more money and hands on experience. When Jim wasn't around,

I quickly realized those cheers to his face were jeers behind his back. Did he have a volatile temper? Yes. We were all under extreme amounts of stress. There were millions of dollars of retail we had to sell and millions in profit that had to be reflected!

All the sales associates befriended Jim and spent substantial time with him at the store and his large homes on the lake. Carole was a middle-aged blonde, single, no kids, and addicted to plastic surgery. Hey, I'm all for kicking Father Time butt! I am just illustrating character. One would think they were best friends. Carole had a vile mouth that showed no mercy to anyone. She produced high profit deals and a client base that reached back over 20 years. One morning, I let Jim know gently that the energy changes when he exits the building. To my surprise he said, "I'm aware." "Oh, okay. I just thought as your friend I had to say something." He really appreciated me doing so. He often mentioned what a good person I was and inquired about who reared me. "My grandmother Aleis". Jim asked me my career goals. "I want to be a successful entrepreneur maybe own my own dealership." Jim said to successfully run a dealership I need to learn every aspect or at least fully understand a particular department and really understand its purpose and how to capitalize on it. "Most importantly you must sell cars." I thought no way! I am not going to be a car saleswoman. Yeah, no thank you I thought to myself. Later that evening when Jim left, I met with two Arabian brothers. I negotiated and sold two warranty policies for their 7-series vehicles. Tom came in the office, sat down and began to tell me what a great job I was doing with clients, but he needed more help with his paperwork. I thought to myself, "Frankly, Tom. I don't give a damn." I whispered softly. "Duly noted." Later that week on Friday night, Nick and I had a dinner date. We debriefed our day. I gave my initiative feelings about Tom and our brief conversation. Tom was the messenger. Tony Jr. and I talked that same day about my work Tony Jr. had me do some correspondence work for the owner, his father Tony Sr. I didn't think mean of it and most certainly was going to give it much more mental energy. Monday comes around and I come in my usual benevolent self and proceed to work. Around lunchtime, Jim revealed to me that the store is super busy and he is bringing on his old finance partner to help us out. He says she is great and I'm going to love her because she is the Italian version of me. My schedule nor payment plan changes. "When does she start?" Wednesday! Told ya. Tom was the messenger or soft nudge. Jim was right. Casey was laid back, hilarious, and positive as the Italian me. This dynamic of the four of us continued for about 6 months.

Jim, Casey and I took a business trip to the financial head-quarters for a few days. We flew that Saturday afternoon and did what we had to do and returned Monday. Jim even made it in for his weekly meeting with Tony Jr. and Tony Sr. He briefly told me about the pain he was in from chronic back spasms and the pain suppressants he used daily. He told the whole staff at some point or another. The managers and owner meeting adjourned Jim tells me there are too many people in the finance department and I am going to have to go on the sales floor. He insisted that he would train me and make sure I would make more than being the finance processor and warranty consultant. He said how imper-ative selling cars would be if I wanted to be a finance director. I expressed that I was losing sight of my original purpose of even working there. No, this is exactly the best way to get acclaimed with clients and comfortable with negotiating effectively and directly. "You're not selling Pontiacs. Most of these vehicles cost more than the average person's home." Sold! He was good. He sold me a career. I immediately started product knowledge train-ing and took the floor that Saturday. Remember how I said the sales associates were nice to me? That changed exponentially. If looks could kill and catty comments could cut, I'd be dead. I was given "the launcher" desk, it was called that because anyone who was assigned there was fired within 3 months.

The jitters arrive on Saturday morning. I wasn't used to waking up so early on a Saturday let alone to work. I put on a crisp white blouse, black slacks and black patent pumps simple yet chic. A brief meeting is held. We clap it out.

When I get to my desk, my phone rings. A man with a thick accent is on the line. All I could understand was the stock number so I searched our database. The car was available and I scheduled an appointment for noon. Since that was only a few hairs away, I went to get the car and pull it out front. En route upstairs, an older gentleman with his son and I exchanged pleasantries. He proceeded to ask me to show him sport utility vehicles. I took them upstairs with me and started off with the benefits of the smaller SUV and moved along to the bigger one. I went through the main purpose, budget, etc.

Finally drove the smaller one alongside the bigger one. Small talk was exchanged on the test drive and we met back up at my desk. They say we want the bigger one in black exterior and brown interior. My porter aka assistant finds it and brings the car over. They ask for a discount and I ask them with dismay on my face: Why? This is the last one we have with color combination and only nine in the entire country. The father's demeanor got a little more aggressive. So, I excused myself and told him let me see what I could do. I went in the back and ate a salad; came back and told him the best I could do is save him the shipping cost he would have to pay if he purchased out of state. He nodded, offered his hand and said "Deal!" I prepped his paperwork and got finance to sign his paperwork and take ownership of his SUV. While father and son were in that process, my noon appointment showed up. His vehicle of interest was already outside. Easy access. Test drive and trade appraisal was all that needed to take place. Easy does it so I thought. Wrong! This guy thought he had the Taj Mahal of trades and wanted top dollar. So basically, my pre-own manager and myself had to devalue his chandelier on wheels and bring him down to reality. We took a little money off the selling price and gave him a little more for his trade-in and we got a deal! All parties were happy. Both clients were sealed and dealed!

After my back to back deals, I went to get some coffee. On my way back, an older black gentleman dressed to the nines held the door for me. "Thank you so much. That's a beautiful three-piece suit. Zegna?" "Yes, how do you know?" "The cut and pattern. It's my boyfriend's go-to designer." "Do you work here?" "I do. What brings you in?" "It's my wife's birthday next week and she wants a red convertible." "Well, let's give the misses what she wants!" The gentleman turned out to be a world-famous pastor.

The pastor had genuine interest and smiles over stories of my childhood in the choir and my grandmother being president of the tithing committee. He settled on a beautiful bright re coup/ convertible. No haggling and he paid cash. His only request was on a extra set of floor mats. By 5 p.m., my feet hurt. I was exhausted. Jim and Tony Jr. called me into the office and began to clap. I was so confused. My face must have expressed that because they both said you have no idea what you did today. As confused as I was, my co-workers were 10 times more confused. They started whispering that Jim and Tony Jr. were throwing me clients. Totally false. I got my pay outs slips and realized I made $7,000 in 8 hours! I still have my first pay out slips. I continued to dominate from "The Launcher" desk for a little over six months before Tony Jr. launched me to the best seat on the floor right by the front door! There was so much floor traffic on some days that I would hide. Our store was three floors of inventory and three off-site warehouses. Productively procrastinating is what I labeled it. If I'm going to dodge dollars, I must maximize another area. Carole was extremely knowledgeable in this area. Jim really campaigned to get her promoted to new car manager. After 9 months consecutively in the top 3 sales associates at the store, I decided to reward myself like any 20-something would by building and buying a $150,000 car. I've always had nice cars, but I designed this one based off Christian Louboutin, my favorite shoe designer. It was black, high gloss metallic with blood red interior.

Around Halloween time, Jim threw a fabulous party at his house on the lake. A lot of people were there including some co-workers. I got so drunk I laid in a coffin and took a picture. Jim, Carole, and I along with 20 or so co-workers all took a shot together in Jim's game room and bar. Jim was fired 9 days later. I remember it so vividly. He went upstairs to Tony Sr.'s office for a meeting like usual. Jim came downstairs and started packing up his belongings. I quickly went into his office to see what was happening. He told me he just got let go. He didn't tell me why and I didn't pry. I just thanked him for all his help and went to the ladies room to cry.

Everything I understood didn't need to be said. I understood Tony Jr. hired me not Jim. I was put on the sales floor with the expectancy to be hung by my own rope and Casey was brought in to replace me. Didn't pan out that way. I continued to build clientele and consecutively stayed in the top three in sales for the following 3 years. The cross I beared was immense. There were 10 sales associates: one solely got all the new car internet leads and was number one every single month even when he went on vacation. Second place was a lady who got every pre-own lead via internet. My only advantage was having a desk by the door and a few rich friends.

People thought Jim was sending me clients because of the time we would spend together working. He was small, but he was like my security guard. SO many people would come in off the street to catcall and harass me. Jim, along with some of the other guys, would always come to my rescue.

I began my deals with Carole and befriended her. One lunch outing, she revealed to me that it was her that told Tony Sr. she felt uncomfortable working with Jim because of his cocktail of pain pills, conceal and carry gun, and anger issues. I will never forget the hate and envy in her eyes when she said, "that motherfucker was making way too much money." The envy and calculation ripped open my old wounds of betrayal. Jim was instrumental in her getting a promotion and a six figure raise. This is how she thanked him. It was turning toxic, so I decided to plan a tropical vacation to Miami with my family followed by Europe with peers: Germany to race on the Autobahn and then venture to Paris. I needed to reevaluate and recalibrate my intentions. After a spa day with my sister, we sat on the tropical sand sipping fruity drinks and eating fish tacos just decompressing.

It came to me so clearly to put an exclamation mark at end of every moment after every encounter, be it perceived as negative or positive. When you have a positive experience, appreciate it and take that energy up a notch to celebrate the celebration! Most importantly do this internally! Darkness is necessary in life because how would we know light? When light is too bright bothersome, it's sometimes unbearable.

My older sister found joy and success in the childcare industry. It suited her nurturing and laid-back personality. We are opposites career wise yet one in the same. Our grandmother lost her battle with ovarian cancer. Grandma Aleis was our rock and her passing shattered us. Both of us needed a getaway. It was great. I came back to work for a week before heading off to Europe. A co-worker asked if I was out for breast augmentation since my D cup went to a DD cup. That was just one irregularity going on with my body. My appetite would disappear for days; my libido would fluctuate; and I would experience great fatigue. This went back once again to my contraceptive. After medical advice and my own research, I switched brands once again.

Off to Europe, our first stop was our headquarters and plant. Nick and I met a client and friend of mine to witness the building of their vehicle and to drive other models on the

Autobahn. Amazing experience and loads of fun! Germany knows how to party and we learned that very quickly. Obviously historical sites were plentiful. Off to the city of lights, Paris! My former boss Francois gave me a list of things to do that were off-beaten path. This was and is his home. Despite warnings, Parisians were nice to me. It was so much to see. I wanted to stay longer. This was my first of several trips here. Maybe I'll write a book in detail about all my many travels.

I returned to work with a sense of gratitude. I had a great appreciation for the co-workers that did bring a genuine smile and laughter to my day. I made sure I took my loved ones out to nice dinners and shows to express gratitude for their contribution to my life even if all they did was call to check on me and say "Hi."

My mindset was laser-focused at work. I knew if I did my best, my next step would come to me organically. I excelled with our high-end clientele for three reasons. One, I undersold and over delivered. It's an extremely factual-based technique. When you verbalize a summary of product and numbers and showcase every benefit and capability. Talk is cheap: show, prove, and wow. That leads me to number two: wow with knowledge and become a ninja in your industry and with your product. A client will be honored to be working with you and will trust you if you are organized and methodical. Word will soon spread, and the sales will come to you. The cherry on top of your wow is your style. Again, present yourself consistently to make the client feel highly regarded just by being in your presence. Number three makes a friend treat a customer, client or potential client with feelings and interest. This is important when gauging the motives for one's actions. Is it a need? A want? An emotional decision?

Our clientele wasn't foreign to me. My clients were professional athletes, TV personalities, Academy Award winning actors and actresses. All my clients got the same service and method. One's economic class did not play a factor. Never judge someone's life by its current view. I've had people come in without a dime to their name and no big casino wins. Their businesses took off. They won court settlements. Men and women were gifted vehicles. Simply hard work and dedicated savings. In short all it takes is one turn of God's favor to turn everything around.

It was 10 p.m. and I was driving on an empty expressway when my phone rang. It was Jim! We kept in touch through the years just checking up on one another. He tells me how he is opening dealerships around the country for some billionaire. He needs a finance director for our state's store and he thinks I'll be perfect! Shut the front door and nail it shut! My first emotion was excitement then fear then back to excitement. I didn't understand my fear it was almost to the point of apprehensiveness. The feeling was unfamiliar to me. What was I afraid of? This was what I wanted, what I manifested: worked towards; screamed "put me in coach" for years for this opportunity. I knew I had to take it. Nick and I planned a quick Vegas getaway prior and I was going to deal with my work life upon my return home. We had had a great time and ended our trip with a bang and by bang, I mean a massive argument. He made it clear that he did not want kids and it broke my heart. I adore children and was always indifferent about having my own until I met him. I wanted Nick's kids. This was non-negotiable and we soon broke up. To this day, he never had children.

Back at the ranch, I was having sleepless nights. Nick and I vowed to remain friends, but it was hard. I had this amazing career opportunity and I was losing someone in a strong, loving capacity. My latest management team was assisting me with making my decision. Tony Jr. was a good general manager and he expanded his vision and business ventures. He has class and flair much like his father. His quiet wisdom can't be taught. Despite that the appointed management team gossiped about him constantly and continued their trend of disloyalty and for that I never respected them on a personal level. However, this was business, a numbers game. If mine added up and matched my calculations, then we good. Life and time have taught me that many mammals don't share this philosophy. Most people want to know the who, what, where, why, when and how of your feelings and if they don't like their findings or don't find answers to the questions that burn them, you're toast to them. I also find myself in Tony Sr. office with our general manager Saadiq. "Promotion?" No, apparently Saadiq conveyed to Tony Sr. that I was spotted driving down the service lane and turned left instead of right, which was the direction of our customer entrance. I turned left to take the truck to a client's office to see if it fitted in his parking spot. I felt this question could've been answered at my desk but whatever. Saadiq then goes into a song and dance about how Georgetta, the finance manager, was upset that I double check the commission on my deals. At this point, I zone out and silently thank God for this nudge. I have and always will encourage anyone to triple check your own and anyone else handlings of your business. The only people that will have a problem with one doing so is someone unsure and if you're unsure, it's because you're unprepared. I caught and prevented so many of her mishaps over time. I felt like I was in the twilight zone. There was mention of time management. I was the top organic seller with no leads!

The guy behind me fetched deals and did good one month, then was gone the next to rehab or therapy, and then back again. He continued this my entire stint. Some others would leave for hours a day to visit their plastic surgeon. Some argue with their spouses on and off all day. One of my co-worker's wife called me accusing me of having an affair with her husband. You know who that was? Saadiq's wife. She was insane. All I know is when I finally spoke, I said thank you for the learning experience and opportunity. I knew that my time of flying below the radar and being above it all had moved me in a new direction. Fear had no place in me anymore. God opened a door and the nudge transformed into a shove. I moved out of Nick's downtown place further north on the lake closer to my new job. I did so with a very heavy heart. I also had many fun memories at my previous job and met some extraordinary people. Tomorrow is a new day and I strongly sensed everything would be better than okay. Jim arranged a meeting with the group directors, me and Michael, the group owner, and star of his own reality show. Prior to our pow wow, I did research on all parties involved and was thoroughly impressed and inspired by Michael's story and purpose. Helping individuals bring their career dreams to fruition.

This ignited a spark within me, giving me direction towards that thing I needed to put my finger on -- the heart and soul of my own business. What Michael did was different than what I had in mind. So many years, I spent with a man I loved that I was certain I was going to marry and spend the rest of my life. Michael had a mansion, a penthouse, beach house, and a "playhouse" (don't ask). So many years I spent traveling the world, making loads of money with some of the world's most interesting and influential people yet almost guilty about it. Financially and socially, I was there for my family. Charity starts with family. However, my business heart and soul plan were to help and assist people in a real way. Doing something I excelled at making and grounding smart and stable career moves.

Today is the day I'm going to meet with Michael. I didn't know what to expect. His financial status didn't faze me. I had several billionaire clients, and some were down to earth. Others had egos that were out of this world. Again, the lessons instilled in me by my grandmother Aleis stuck with me. "It all belongs to God and no one is better than the next. God gives it and he'll take it." Small talk I detest. Interesting uplifting and productive conversing is only allowed through my cerebral cortex. Now let's be clear: God will put a message in a baby or a homeless person. Remain humble enough to receive it.

I meet with the guys and it was laid back almost to the point of comatose. Some guy told me to sell him a pen and I told him my name wasn't Walgreens. Everyone got quiet then laughed. After my briefing with the fellow directors, I received a tour of the facilities. The tour ends and I am seated in an empty office and in comes Michael. He is taller, fit and extremely well groomed. All I wanted to do was tell him that I wasn't reared and cared for by my parents either! I want to assist others with their career goals as well! Too soon Tan. Too soon.

Michael fell into the down to earth category. The task I was entrusted to do was transparent and there was honestly never a doubt in my mind that I could complete it with flying colors. My pay plan was lucrative with a solid base and percentage of sales. The plan promoted productivity yet showed appreciation and gratitude for my talents.

A lot of people fear commission and risk/reward salaries. I would want it no other way. That's the key to unlimited income. I shared my good news with my family and all they acknowledged was the base salary, I knew they would. The pieces fell into place so easily. The clientele was there: inventory, staff, banks. I was in my zone. I had laser focus and that was saving money to invest in my business and nothing, nor anyone, was going to stop me.

I kept ranking top in gross for several years consecutively. The hours were long. Time would fly due to our light and fun atmosphere. Jim got a promotion and hired a familiar face, Jameson, a former Harley Davidson executive and general manager. I previously worked with him at my preceeding place of employment. I always thought he was stylish and cool, so I was pleased to hear about his acquisition. The two current managers did not share my enthusiasm. Dan and Mohammed were suburban guys that viewed us as ritzy city slickers. Jameson would pay cash for his cars at the store. He never bought any vehicle under 160k and to this day rode the prettiest Harley I've ever seen. That drove Dan and Mohammed insane.

I don't know how they got wind of my pay plan. All I know is Jameson approached me about it saying mine was the only one set up this way. A new plan was figured out where I would make even more money. False. I crunched those numbers against our average traffic, and the numbers came out slightly less with me working longer and harder. Umm no, that's not what I agreed on. They basically tried to Jim me from our previous job, but they had nothing on me. I'm a mild-mannered people person who delivers. I stood my ground and they left me alone. If they have nothing on you, they can't do anything to you. Except try to give you a headache. It was white noise to me: laser focus, save to invest in my dream. I was a double minority and was reminded of that a few times. Nevertheless, my tried and true approach is to be so good and leave no room for error. Unfortunately, we live in a world whereas some people have a problem with either or both. My advice to minorities is whatever services, talent or gift you are presenting: be so phenomenal that there is no room for nothing but respect at the very least. For over two years, I hit a consistent lateral profit margin for my location. This came naturally to me. The relationship building with banks; gaining mass profit; gaining respect from employees and clients.

Word obviously started to spread of the job I was doing because I got a visit at our location from the lawyer of two brothers that owns a dealership. They really wanted to meet with me to discuss an opportunity to work for several large brands under one umbrella with extensive training, phenomenal pay and travel to locations that actually excited me. I suffer chronic wanderlust.

I was so swamped at my current position that we scheduled a phone interview. I took the phone call in a meditation room. Before any important communication, I like to meditate and pray. I did just that and then my phone rang. The call lasted about 30 minutes. While I was on the call, I emailed my monthly logs showcasing my profits. By the end of the 30-minute conversation, I was asked to start immediately. My first mission, if I chose to accept it, would be at the Vanderbilt estate in South Carolina in a matter of a few weeks for seminar and to demonstrate team building. Climbing the corporate ladder was an understatement. I was skyrocketing up and collecting all the fuel and ammo I needed for my own battleship mission accepted. The Vanderbilt compound was beautiful. After a very whimsical lunch by the lake, I began to miss Nick. I'm sure by this time he had moved on and my laser focus has caused my dating life to suffer immensely. I decided to write Nick a letter. Oddly enough, I travel with stationery.

When writing my letter, I noticed the letters looked blurry to me. I rubbed my eyes and then the lettering looked fine again. I went back to my room to prepare for the meeting I had to conduct. While reading client bios, once again, the lettering became blurry to me. I decided to get some rest and get an early start in the morning.

I woke up bright eyed and bushy tailed. Prepped for my day and knocked the ball out the park. It was a successful first endeavor. Back to our office base for a few weeks. I made an appointment with the optometrist for an eye exam (that blurry vision disturbed me). My exam revealed that I had 20/20 vision.

The optometrist suggested low prescription contact lenses to assist with reading. The lenses were ready right in time for my Sweden trip. This flight stands out to me due to its delays and poor service. The flight was pushed back so many times the airline gifted me a free future flight anywhere of my choice. I was running a day behind when I arrived at one of our brands headquarters in Stockholm, Sweden. I checked into my hotel, showered, changed clothes, and got the car service to meet our team. Just a strategic meeting and unveiling of our new vehicle followed by product competitive comparison demonstrating.

Everything went fine in the morning. After lunch, I broke out in a sweat and felt extremely lightheaded. I didn't want to alarm anyone so I excused myself to hydrate with water and ginger ale. I returned in time to drive and compare some unreleased luxury automobiles.

I'm in this foreign country by myself with no knowledge of the healthcare system. There was no room or time for me to freak out. I found a quiet corner and began to pray. I knew I had control over my mind. No matter what is going on the mind must be grounded and calm even when you have a tornado in your stomach and a hurricane in your head. Just as I finished praying, I rejoined my team and an overcast made its presence in the sky, a loud thunder was released, and it began to pour down raining. It lasted for several hours. Our driving session was scheduled outside with a world-famous race car driver that everyone was excited about. I never heard of him. Wouldn't be able to pick him out of a lineup.

I took in a few shops and headed back to my room to take a power nap before our banquet dinner. Dressed to progress and ready to be done with this dinner. After a few colorful words from the brands CEO, dinner was followed by a cocktail reception. I mingled and found my seat. Right next to a man that stood about 5'11", silver blue eyes and well-defined bone structure (his face was chiseled). He was walking and talking on a cell phone and sat next to me. He continued to talk in what appeared to be Italian for a few moments and dismissed the call. He turned around and our eyes met.He spoke to me in English with a heavy sexy accent. I told him my name and where I was from. He did the same mentioning he travels a lot as well and never mentioning what he does for a living. My exit strategy turned into a conversation about our favorite restaurants, chefs around the world, and socialism. He asked me if I wanted to leave to go get a drink. I politely declined. We were in a hall with three open bars leaving with him to get drinks only meant one thing. I didn't care how hot he was. It's not that easy with me, sorry signore! I was fighting back the piece of bread I ate for dinner from making a second appearance.

There was only room for one in my bed. Awakened nice and early to burn some rubber on the road! Gassed up on orange juice and vitamin C. I felt great! Maybe five shiny cars were lined up. All equal value by different brands. It was my duty to drive them around a racetrack and then explain extensively why one was better than the rest. Yes, I flew halfway around the world and got compensated well to do so. A few words from a guy with a metal helmet; standing beside a concept racing car, he removes his helmet and low and behold it was the silver fox from the previous night. He buckled up and took off so fast his race car became a sound. I've never seen anyone drive like that in my life. It was such a rush to simply watch. After the demonstration it was my turn to give my selection a few laps around the track. I began to drive the first automobile delicately. By the fifth lap, I was flooring the gas pedal. "Caution meet the wind!" When I parked the car back, I was met with a solo applause and the whitest teeth I've ever seen. All I could think was God is a dramatic orchestrator who clearly likes to see me take huge gambles with my love life. I told him I was leaving first thing in the morning and he was departing later that night for Spain. Until next time. Handshakes were firm and reached everyone. I proceeded to hightail back to my hotel to change for dinner. I told the silver fox he had the matter of hours to make me fall in love with him. He replied "I can make you fall in love in minutes." Cleanup in aisle seven: bring a mop and sponges. We met for dinner and had a great evening filled with laughs and good food. He shared cute stories about his children, pets, and voyages. We discussed our future travel plans and vowed to meet up very soon at one of his upcoming races and ended the night with a kiss.

I had a great time. As soon as the airplane wheels touched Chicago, a warm peace came over me. Nothing like a warm Midwest bear hug of friendliness and brisk wind. As I was changing lanes, I noticed my distance perception was off. I was wearing my contacts yet still experiencing vision challenges. I phoned my older sister to let her know I landed safely and to spill our guts. Her birthday was approaching quickly. As a treat I told her I'll take her wherever she wanted to go in the world. I knew what she would say "New York City." Yes, a 2-hour flight away. She simply wanted her favorite Chinese food and to take in a Broadway play, done and done.

Second order of business schedule an appointment with an ophthalmologist. The optometrist was clearly putting a band-aid over a larger issue. The lovely scheduler that serenaded me with loud chewing gum popping and tons of sass gave me the earliest appointment available 6 months out.

Back at the office, I had to interview and fill two positions and finalize financial reports. I conducted 16 interviews in one day and it was common for me to leave work at 11 p.m. with a start time of 10 a.m. My head was spinning. My body was ready for the spa induced weekend I planned for Kiki's birthday weekend in New York City. We arrived in the evening to fireworks in Central Park where we were staying. We chowed down at chows per usual.

We danced at the rooftop lounge at our hotel and ended our night with our hotel race ritual. What's our hotel race ritual, you ask? My sister and I find the longest and empty hall and race back to the room running top speed. Loser buys breakfast. Sometimes I win. This time Kiki won. She did run track in school. The spa was everything I needed. It was followed by a stroll through Central Park.

It was a beautiful autumn day. The kind of day you just sit outside and take in the earth. The natural gifts God bestowed upon us. "Ouch! something is really irritating my left eye." I thought to myself. I purchased eye drops from the pharmacy right before the play we were attending. I put a few drops in en route to the show. Our driver dropped us off at the complete opposite end of the block. We were speedwalking to our destination and my eye was still irritated, so I put in a few more eye drops. We arrive right in time. We take our seats and I couldn't open my eye without experiencing pain. My sister and I creeped out to the ladies room to look. My sister was a few steps behind. The eye looked fine except for excess water. I rinsed my eye with water and the water made it sting. I had to leave and go to the emergency clinic. To be honest, the show we selected was terrible. Maybe my eye was simply rejecting bad theatre. I enter the clinic, explained what was going on. The doctor saw me right away. He examined my eye with a light and had me read the eye chart and count his fingers. He determined that my eye was irritated from too many eye drops. Told me to stop using them and get a good night rest and my eye should feel better in the morning.

In the morning, like magic, my eye felt better. I wasn't satisfied and made an appointment with my primary physician the following week back home. I told her about my recent events. She asked me "are you under stress?" Not really, I replied. I provided my day in the life schedule for the previous month.

I felt great. I just had these vision changes; my doctors only concern was my high blood pressure. I was prescribed a low dosage medication and took a laundry list of blood tests that all came back negative. Something just didn't feel right to me. So far, I've had three doctors tell me I am fine. They can't find anything wrong with me. Whether I have clear vision for a day was a crap shoot. I did my own research. Doctors study medicine and practice health. All three doctors had the same "I can't find anything wrong" phrase. Something was wrong. My body was screaming "something is wrong." They simply couldn't find it. I compiled a list of over 400 reasons that could cause inconsistent foggy vision and depth perception problem. I continuously removed those with symptoms that didn't apply. I ended up with a list of over 20 diagnoses. I had a trip planned with my family that weekend. As I walked through the airport, my vision was so foggy that I bumped into two people. We were coming back from an exhibit at The Artist formerly known as Prince's house in Minnesota. We landed in the afternoon. By nightfall, I went to the emergency room determined that I am not leaving until someone tells me what is wrong with me and I meant it!!

It was oddly crowded for a Sunday evening. That's what a nurse told me. After a few hours of waiting, I had an ekg, vitals, and getting hit on by a guy in a wheelchair and vomit on his shirt. Then it was my turn to speak with the doctor. For what seemed like the hundredth time, I explained my symptoms and

I ended up counting doctor fingers and reading eye exam charts. With the doctor saying everything looks fine. "Doc, it's not fine. My depth perception is off, my peripheral is closing in and my foggy vision is anything but fine. I have an appointment within 6 months, but this issue is pressing. I have a list of 20 diagnoses with my symptoms and I am not leaving this hospital until I am diagnosed and treated." I was given a room and within 30 minutes, an older man and middle-aged woman said they were the head doctors on duty. Oddly enough she was holding my diagnosis that I compiled. The previous doctor gave it to her. She asked me to stand up and walk in a straight line several times. I was asked whether I had been experiencing headaches? I have not been experiencing headaches. After several straight-line strolls, I became unbalanced. She looked me in the eye and suspected a nerve issue. They ordered an MRI of my brain right away.

I was giving patient attire and inserted into a capsule like apparatus. The tech asked me what kind of music did I want. Prince please!! Felt like Eternity. I just prayed. I prayed myself to sleep. I was taken back to my room. The doctor ordered me a spinal tap. I seem to have a pseudo tumor. "The spinal tap will confirm that and indicate your cerebral fluid pressure level. Let me explain: a pseudo tumor is also referred to as idiopathic intercranial hypertension. Our brain lives in and need constant fluid from our body that travels up through our spinal cord from our lower spine to the brain. When the pressure of that fluid is raised, the spinal fluid wreaks havoc on the nerves causing intolerable headaches and vision loss. Why vision loss you ask? The optic nerves consist of a gazillion wire like nerves that connect from the brain to the eye, extending about 9 centimeters and directly in the pathway of overflowing spinal fluid. Idiopathic intercranial hypertension aka pseudo tumor beats up the optic nerves causing them to swell up. Once the swelling is brought down, your baseline vision is revealed aka what's left of your eyesight. During the entire horrible disease, your retinal gangloid cells are dying; causing your optic nerves to go atrophic disabling vision to travel through only damaged optic nerve. Severity ranging from sight vision loss to complete blindness."

The sun peeked from the window while two young doctors stood over me. One oddly attractive and flirty. He starts explaining the procedure of spinal tap; a long measuring needle indicates the pressure. A second component is added to that same needle to remove the excess fluid and lowering the fluid pressure.

When I was informed I indeed have a pseudo tumor, I felt a sense of relief. All the time doctors were looking at the eye.

The issue was behind the eye. I finally got diagnosed. I finally got my answers.

Idiopathic means arising spontaneously from an obscure or unknown source. It's like you're being chosen by an invisible moody monster, not knowing what pissed it off. Possible causes for young women: stress; birth contraceptives; irregular body mass index. Treatment varies based on severity and teamwork. I knew I had to do my part. I expectedly discontinued all contraceptives; lightened my 12-hour workday and hired a nutritionist. I got a prescription. I was released into the wild. My vision cleared up perfectly after the spinal tap.

I informed some peers that I will be transferring to our downtown Chicago location and becoming more involved with the hiring process. Brief best describes the details I shared about my health. Reactions ranged from tear-filled private uplifting speeches to others asking how I was feeling followed by "hey, who's getting your office?" or "may I have your fan?"

I'm back in the big city location once again at a fishbowl building. Stunning location: our service center was adjacent to our office building. One day while I was conversing with an employee, I noticed a chandelier on wheels pull into the service drive and out steps Carlos. Right away we locked eyes, I simply wave and smile. Forgiving those that never ask to be forgiven. Is done within and you don't have to let those transgressors back into your life. The oddest thing started happening every few days he was at my job. He did get drafted in the first round. I don't know if he was having a slow off season or what, but he began befriending my staff, hanging out in the gift shop always dressed picturesquely. Speaking of pictures, my service valet caught him look at my social media while waiting around, another co-worker he befriended told me he talks fondly about me.

It was extremely odd and childish. He kept popping up everywhere I was at and befriending people I knew, trying to make me come to him. It got weird when he requested me on social media. No big deal. I accepted. I looked around his page a little bit and kept on with my day. I got a request from his brother, best friend, sister, and sister in law. One day during his off season, Carlos shows up with his best friend to inquire about buying a car. He was assigned a specialist, yet no sell. The very next day, his best friend was sitting in his car outside my office window, I ignored him. It's a free country, I don't own the street. The very next day, he was there. When I walked over to take a picture, he sped off. I began getting to walk to my car. Honestly, I was scared. Why was this happening and how dare he even show his face after stealing my wallet years before. There is light and dark in us all creating a gray area. It's up to us individually to decide the dark -- we can tolerate games and unnecessary lies are non-negotiable.

That would've worked on a 20-year-old. Unlike many, I didn't just get older. I grew wiser. I've also been blessed to be loved and cared for by some great guys and their actions were never inherent. Great stats, plaques, knowing and partying with celebrities' triggers absolutely nothing within on an emotional base. I know there is a truly magnificent man for me, and I will not settle. Settling brings out your lower vibrations, boredom, jealousy, envy, and flat out misery. Operating on your highest vibration should always be the goal.

July 17, 2017 is a day I will never forget. No, not for mentioning the holy number and my lucky number seven 3 ties 7-17-17. My life began to turn no flip upside down. It all began Sunday, July 16, 2017. I woke up early to a bright beautiful day. I sat on my balcony, drank some tea and planned my day. Got dressed and departed for church; the preacher told the story of Joseph. It has always been one of my favorites. I then completed my grocery shopping and meal planning cooking for the week. I boiled a big pot of cabbage with honey and ginger. Slow cooked and broiled a chicken with garlic, turmeric, and my secret spices.

I also made my signature surf and turf Caesar salad to start the week. By this time, it was late afternoon and time for my beauty break. What's my beauty break you ask? It's when I detox my skin and take nap. Awakened refreshed and ready to get dressed for a friend's party. The atmosphere was a savvy evening pool soiree. A co-worker texted me to come hang out with and some other managers and clients. This was the normal since we all had become friends. My time here was winding down. I like to make an impact and retract. So, I leave and head over to meet up with my work friends. When I arrived, they were already having what I call an Irish speakeasy! I'm 20% Irish so I can say that. The cause for celebration? Our international director was leaving the company and wanted us to know first. He got an amazing opportunity and was leaving expeditiously. We laughed, joked and told stories until the lounge lights came on. Our cars were outside lined up. The fun continued outside. Someone asked me to make a toast since I was the only one who had not been drinking. It was me, Victor, Al, Matt, and Ethan, who was leaving. I made them raise their drinks and said blessings and to make room for bigger blessings. This is not a goodbye: more like "I'll see you around" but not as often and whatever void that caused you to seek fulfillment elsewhere. I speak for all of us in wishing you nothing but the best! After my toast, I put on my designated driver hat. Not before long, I attempted to change lanes on Lake Shore Drive and a car almost sideswiped me. Victor soon said "Is it me or are we swerving?" The guys then started joking about my driving. Mind you I have always been an excellent driver. I hadn't had a cocktail in months. The laughs were silenced when I was merging to exit, derailed off the exit and ended up in the park. Passengers and the vehicle unscathed. I literally gathered myself together and drove off the grass. All asked "What the heck happened?" I misgauged the exit. My peripheral is off. Victor suddenly looked and sounded sober and said, "We have to get you to the hospital or you're going to end up hurt or dead out here." A car full of party animals drove to urgent care at the hospital. I signed in and they all waited for me. For the first time, I felt a heightened fear. I saw the fear and worry in their eyes. I felt it in their energy. I thanked them profusely and dismissed them when I was called in by the doctor. I told the doctor what transpired, and he ordered an emergency spinal tap. He made me stay through the night to see the ophthalmologist.

First thing in the morning, the spinal tap revealed my spinal fluid was elevated and that my medication was failing me. I woke up with my head and vision in a cloud. I was delivered in a wheelchair by department staff to the opthomologist. This hospital is massively huge with several buildings and bridges.

I was rolled to the front desk of the department and walked to the waiting area for a few moments. Dr. Rogers, an extremely loud-spoken man in his upper 60's or lower 70's, arrived. Tall and thin, Dr. Rogers took a x-ray of my optic nerves. He quickly noticed I was losing vision from the peripheral moving inward. One eye being worst than the other. He advised an emergency surgery to save as much of my vision as possible and explained two surgical procedures to me. Option 1 and his suggestion: an optic nerve fenestration. The procedure entails cutting a small pathway behind the eye stopping the fluid from strangling the optic nerve and sending the fluid into the orbit. Option 2 was a brain shunt. Full out brain surgery that implants a hose-like instrument in the brain that flows on the side of the neck, down the chest and releasing the spinal fluid into the stomach. Either would be performed right away. I obviously had a big decision to make in a small amount of time. I excused myself to make some phone calls. All family were called to get their opinion and support. I didn't want to worry them; I knew they would want to be there for me. I was on the phone, I overheard Dr. Rogers telling "we are going to have to perform an emergency surgery on a gal here today, if we don't, she is going to go blind!" I literally ran down the hall crying my eyes out.

Family came to the hospital. Option 1 was the surgery I decided upon. I was assigned a hospital suite and waited for an operating room to become available. My family and I met the surgical team and got another rundown. My family felt at ease. I knew the only thing would put us as ease would be my spirit so I continued to be my usual joyous self. I was scared and unraveling on the inside so I found my inner strength in my spirituality. I prayed constantly to God and truly believed this was all happening for a reason that superseded my understanding at the moment. There was one person missing: my sister. She was on her way from her boyfriend and FaceTime to make the surgeons stall until she got there. She made it right when I was being rolled to the operating room. We embraced with tears in our eyes and it was lights out for me. I woke up hours later with a patch over my eye and a chipped front tooth due to complications from the breathing tube. The hospital immediately issued funds for my dental repair. The lead surgeon Dr. Priya gave the premise that the spinal fluid will no longer cause vision damage and save my remaining vision. Worst case scenario my nerves reveal swollen and my vision drops. I was released with a swollen eye, chipped front tooth, and a mind full of uncertainty. I was instructed to rest and not stress. Hard thing to do with an eye swelled three times its size and diminishing vision. My vision worsened as my swelling decompressed. I frantically called around to get a second opinion. Visiting other doctors and all opinions led to emergency brain surgery. I was in an internal flux. I would sit on my balcony look at the stars in the sky all night praying for answers, praying for guidance. Pray for vision.

I had 4weeks of Dr. Rogers advising me to give the surgery a chance to heal. The waiting became unbearable as my world and vision continued to close in on me. It was Saturday night. I was watching a movie and I felt a quick pinch in my left eye and immediately knew something bad happened. The eyesight in my left eye dropped drastically and was rushed to the hospital where I was told that I must undergo brain surgery. My doctor's words were "I really wanted to avoid this, but we must take a more aggressive approach." Here I go again with another emergency surgery. I checked into my hospital suite with Kiki. Changed into my gown and waited for a plan of action. Dr. Favas was the first surgeon to visit me. His responsibility was to make sure the cord properly flowed to and through my stomach seamlessly leaving no scars. Shortly after, Dr. Dotts and his entourage came to me. He is the rock star of neurosurgery. The man has long wavy hair and a beautiful face and body. He entered the room in a cloud of smoke, muscles peeking out of his smock and an entourage of about 15 doctors.

These surgical briefings began to feel like déjà vu. The surgical team stood around my room as neurosurgeons explained the intricate procedure and its risk. I anticipated him opening the floor for my questions and obviously my first one was: will I regain the vision I have lost thus far? "This procedure will get you to your baseline." Baseline? "Let me break getting damaged optic nerves caused by swelling to baseline. It's like fixing a flat tire with fix a flat. The damaged tire is the optic nerve and the fix a flat is the swelling holding the vision. When the fix a flat is emptied, you'll still have a tire, but it will be damaged, and you won't know how badly until it is emptied to its baseline." Up until this point I felt like I was immersed in the most intense déjà vu humanly possible.

The optic nerve fenestration on was supposed to be my saving grace and yet I feel that procedure opened the flood gates. My vision is drowning. Legions of doctors and surgeons are racing against time to save and resuscitate what remains. My hospital room was brisk and began to fill with plants, flowers, and family. The conversations remained current-event based and relaxed. I could see the worry in their eyes and body language. After a few hours of prepping and waiting, showtime. I was rolled down and met with the anesthesia team and then parked in my same bed. In the corner behind a curtain, Kiki was initially the only person allowed in the operating area with me. We talked about all the music festivals we've attended in the past: Coachella and Lollapalooza that we missed just months ago due to my health tribulations. Three younger surgeons pulled the curtain back and introduced themselves. I could tell by one's accent that he was from eastern Europe; the other two Lebanese on their pronunciation of Muhammad. Every eastern country says it slightly different. They pull chairs around my bed in silence with very stern looks on their faces. Once looked extremely pensive to the point of concealing great anger in silence. However, it was escaping through his eyes. He inched closer and closer never breaking eye contact or his silence when he finally said "I am on your operating team and I was standing on the other side of your curtain and I too am very upset. I am extremely upset to be exact." "And why is that?" Without hesitation, he replied because "Beyoncé got pregnant and cancelled her Coachella performance and my fiancé also got pregnant so no Coachella for me either." You came in here like you were the Grimm reaper all because you want to hear *Single Ladies* by Beyoncé." Laughter from an audience from outside emerged. I asked my sister to pull the curtains back and simply blown away by the large staff operating staff congregating around me. I began to weep uncontrollably because I could feel my world getting smaller as my vision worsened. I felt a thunder in my belly, a hurricane in my throat and a flood in my head and it all erupted in a thunderous cry and screaming. "I can't live without my eyesight, why is this happening to me? Dear God, what did I do to deserve this?" Subconsciously, these questions have been festering. I was baptized as a baby: started Bible study at age 4; joined church choir at 5 and spent just about every weekend learning how to love God, be a good Christian and a good person. I was promised that Jesus would light my path and guide me along the way. Well my path is getting dimmer and dimmer and has led me in the arms of a stranger. Dr. Falk was consoling me and telling me he and the staff are here for me and that I did absolutely nothing wrong. I began to ask even more questions: How long is the procedure? Depends, anywhere from 2-6 hours. What area of the brain can be affected? I was assured not to worry the shunt will be implanted in a small area that does not affect functionality. It will be placed in the area that controls seizures. Should I expect physical pain after the surgery? There will be a pain level it just depends on your tolerance level. My Q & A session was interrupted with "we're ready to begin now." The remaining of my family came down to support me and I'll never forget as I was being rolled away, a young female doctor slightly kneeled at my bed and said doctors and scientists are working diligently all around the world for a cure for optic nerve damage. They are getting closer and closer using stem cells and other methods. She smiled and said it's coming soon! I went into anesthesia and came out 5 hours later in a fog and sporting a mohawk. I was rolled outside of my operating room and waiting to be brought back upstairs along with Dr. Mohammad. As soon as I opened my eyes, I was taken back on how different my surrounding look. Dr. Rockstar emerged to check on me before I headed up and I described to him my vision, the dimming, and fogginess.

He informed me that inducing medication exposed the baseline of my senses. "Dear God, this can't be", I thought to myself as I was rolled to my room and he smiled and waved sweetly to me. I get to my bedroom and was pleasantly surprised to find loved ones from wall to wall. The room smelled amazing due to all the gorgeous flowers. However, I was in so much pain physically and emotionally. I just wanted pain pills and a nap. It felt so good to be surrounded by so much love. I haven't felt this much love since I was 4 years old. As soon as my head hit the pillow, a nurse entered to do maintenance work on me. I quickly rose to my feet and walked away with her. I came out and my aunt said, "I can leave now because I witnessed a miracle, my niece just had brain surgery and stood up and moved quicker than me." I fell asleep and woke up to a doctor and aide standing over me to take me to get my shunt checked. The doctor stuck a needle filled with dark fluid; he sticks the needle in the shunt in the back of my head to see if the fluid from my spinal fluid was now flowing quickly and properly. I was rolled back to my room and slept to the morning. Once again, I awakened to pills on a platter. A knock on the door from Dr. Rockstar surprised me. He asked to enter. I allowed clearance and he sat down and made himself comfortable and man spread like he had been traveling through the night to deliver a message. He asked how I was feeling? I'm okay, considering possibly going blind I thought. However, I replied "fine, thank you for asking." He begins to tell me about a 7-year-old boy who he has operated on 18 times; a 6-month-old baby who he has performed brain surgery on four times, and countless spinal taps to nurse her back to health and a pastor of the church who served the church and the community his entire life.

Before shunts were created, people who experienced hydrocephalus simply died. Reviewing your shunt test, we discovered that the cord has a knot and we must perform one more neurosurgery to get everything flowing properly. Your fluid level on your brain was extremely high and I lowered it off the top during your first brain surgery. We got to do what we got to do,

I replied. You take good care of me please. He replied, "I most certainly will take excellent care of you."

Ophthalmology is outside your door. We will perform your surgery at 3:30 p.m. The ophthalmology team entered as he left to check my vision and administer a steroid pill to decompress my swollen optic nerve out a quicker pace.

3:30 p.m. rolled around and my bed was rolled down to the operating room like directly in where Adele was belting out "Hello from the other side." I was put to sleep. I was pumped with pain medication for a few days and soon released to go home.

My family surrounded me with prayer. They were literally fighting over whose home I would be looked after while I heal, chaperone me to doctor appointments, and keep me on suicide watch. Some thought I would hurt myself. Most don't truly know the makeup of my character. Listening is a skill where I am a ninja. The downside is this attracts talkers, selfish talkers. They listen simply with the intention and anticipation to talk, missing the opportunity to truly comprehend. Once I discover you're a selfish conversationist, I give you my ear and eventually their space and echoing of their own voice. Furthermore, I'm just naturally private. Thought my tribulations, I didn't tell one friend. Not one. My life after brain surgeries was me combing the country for a medical team to capitalize on my vision and get it to the best stats of clarity possible.

I ended up with the two best neurologists tag team working from two different hospitals. Both chiefs of neurology. One administering monthly spinal taps; the other a medical treatment of a pill cocktail. As we search ferociously to restore my vision; my Uncle Derrick found a treatment center in Germany that activates your remaining retinal gangloid cells. After living in Germany for a month with my aunt Towanna and an obscene amount of money spent, I waited in immeasurable physical pain and silence hoping and praying for improvement. I became a hermit for nearly 9 months constantly in bed afraid to experience the world as a visually impaired woman. I began to live in my head daydreaming about adventures and land I wanted to explore. Becoming fascinated with volcanoes. The boiling underground and eruption became my latest area of study. I dreamed of going to Hawaii to tour the volcanoes and feeling that magic of the earth. Daydreams of praying at the Vatican and being on the Amalfi Coast in Italy.

Partying with robots, going to the highest point in Japan at Mount Fuji and taking in my favorite current artist Kusama. Visit and help orphans in the Middle East and learn to rock climb. But first, I must get out of this damn bed and find my strength and confidence. Remember who I am and recognize that I'm bent, not broken, and snap back into myself better yet snap back better. Stronger, wiser, loving, grateful, and fearless.

One night while in a deep sleep, I dreamt of my grandmother and grandfather. They were playing with me and I appeared to be around 3. My grandmother picked up 3-year-old me, hugged and kissed my cheeks, and told me to stop letting the pet parrot out of the cage. "Instead set yourself free. You're still the beautiful woman I raised you to be." I woke up crying uncontrollably and the very next morning searched for my notes on the company I wanted to start before I fell ill. With Kiki by my side, I started months of research and business courses and created Fresh Start Assistance, an employment agency for ambitious professionals looking for a fresh start in their career. I am free, Grandma Aleis. I am soaring because you taught me with hope in my heart there is always a chance for a fresh start.

The imperturbable during the storm is when the extinct is reborn shinier and new. Set out and accomplished all that was planned to do. Thankful for the pain for it magnified the joy that was regained and a spirit that sustains.

We all have commonalties based on dreams and reality.

Always take a moment to find the calm in calamity.

In Hawaii at one with the volcanoes.

Baptism on the Amalfi Coast

Retraining to climb in a different and exciting way.

Continuing my love of traveling the world to take in architecture and art in Japan (Kusama Museum)

Mount Fuji, Japan